|||| ||||||||||||||||||||||||||||||||||||||||||||

◁ **W9-BRB-458**

ANIMAL TRACKS
of the
Great Lakes

by Chris Stall

Illinois, Indiana, Michigan, Minnesota,
New York, Pennsylvania, Ohio, Wisconsin,
and Quebec, Ontario

THE
MOUNTAINEERS

To my pal Dave; and to all the other good people who put the heartland into my heart, especially Angela, Anita & Woodie, Ellyn, Karla, Kim, Larry & Loreen, Larry, Linda & Mike, Mary & Remco, Matt, Myra, Sandy & Randy, and Susan.

The Mountaineers: Organized 1906 " . . . to explore, study, preserve, and enjoy the natural beauty of the Northwest."

© 1989 by The Mountaineers
All rights reserved

First printing 1989, second printing 1992, third printing 1994, fourth printing 1997

Published by The Mountaineers
1001 S.W. Klickitat Way, Suite 201, Seattle, Washington 98134

Manufactured in the United States of America

Edited by Cathy Johnson
Book design by Betty Watson
Cover design by Nick Gregoric
Author photo by Angela Staubach
Track on cover: Beaver

No part of this book may be reproduced in any form, or by any electronic, mechanical, or other means, without permission in writing from the publisher.

Library of Congress Cataloging-in-Publication Data
Stall, Chris.
    Animal tracks of the Great Lakes states.

    Bibliography: p.
    Includes index.
    1. Animal tracks—Lake States.   2. Mammals—Lake States.   3. Birds—Lake States.   I. Title.
QL719.L34S72   1989   599.0977   89-3329
ISBN 0-89886-196-9

CONTENTS

Preface

Most people don't get a chance to observe the animals in the wild, with the exceptions of road kills and a few nearly tame species in parks and campgrounds. Many wild animals are nocturnal or scarce, and many are shy and secretive to avoid the attention of predators, or stealthy as they stalk their next meal. In addition, most wild creatures are extremely wary of humans either instinctively or because they've learned through experience to be that way. We may catch fortuitous glimpses now and then, but few of us have the time or motivation required for lengthy journeys into wild country for the sole purpose of locating animals. The result is that areas where we would expect to see animals often seem practically devoid of wildlife.

That's rarely the case, of course. Actually, many animals reside in or pass through all reasonably wild habitats. Though we may not see them, they nevertheless leave indications of their passage. But for the most part such signs are obscure or confusing so that only the most experienced and knowledgeable wilderness travelers notice them.

There's one grand exception: *animal tracks*. Often readily apparent even to the most casual and inexperienced observer, tracks not only indicate the presence of wild animals but can also be matched relatively easily with the animals that made them. I guess that's why I have been fascinated by animal tracks since my childhood in rural New York, and why that focus has continued through two decades of wandering and searching for them in wild lands all across North America.

Animal Tracks of the Great Lakes States is a compilation of many years and many miles of my own field work, protracted observations, sketching, photography, and research into a list of articles and books too long to name and too heavy to carry into the backcountry.

Animal tracks may be something you concern yourself with only when you happen on them, or your interest in tracks may become nearly obsessive. You may find yourself hiking with your chin resting securely on your chest, feverishly scanning the ground for clues. You may seek out snow because tracks show up on it better than

5

most other surfaces. In the absence of snow, you might find yourself altering your routes, avoiding bedrock and ground cover, seeking out damp sand, soft dirt and mud along streams, near ponds and lakes, around swamps. You may journey into the desert in early morning, before the sand dries and moves on the wind. After a rainfall, you might make special trips to check fresh mud, even along dirt roads or hiking trails, knowing that among evidence of human activity the animal prints will be clear and precise.

Whatever your degree of interest, I hope you will enjoy using this book, in your backyard or in the wildest and most remote regions of the Great Lakes states, and that your interest in identifying tracks grows until you reach the level of knowledge at which you no longer need this book.

Good luck!

Chris Stall
Cincinnati, Ohio

Introduction

HOW TO USE THIS BOOK

1. When you first locate an unknown track, look around the immediate area to locate the clearest imprint (see Tracking Tips below). You can usually find at least one imprint or even a partial print distinct enough for counting toes, noting the shape of the heel pad, determining the presence or absence of claw marks, and so on.

2. Decide what kind of animal is most likely to have made the tracks; then turn to one of the two main sections of this book. The first and largest features mammals; the second, much shorter section is devoted entirely to birds.

3. Measure an individual track, using the ruler printed on the back cover of this book. Tracks of roughly five inches or less are illustrated

life-size; those larger than five inches have been reduced as necessary to fit on the pages.

4. Flip quickly through the appropriate section until you find tracks that are about the same *size* as your mystery tracks. The tracks are arranged roughly by size from smallest to largest.

5. Search carefully for the tracks in the size range that, as closely as possible, match the *shape* of the unknown tracks.

6. If you find the right shape but the size depicted in the book is too big, remember that the illustrations represent tracks of an average *adult* animal. Perhaps your specimen was made by a young animal. Search some more: on the ground nearby you might locate the tracks of a parent, which will more closely match the size of the illustration.

7. Read the comments on range, habitat, and behavior, to help confirm the identification.

This book is intended to assist you in making field identifications of commonly encountered animal tracks. To keep the book compact, my remarks are limited to each animal's most obvious characteristics. By all means enhance your own knowledge of these track makers. Libraries and book stores are good places to begin learning more about wild animals. Visits to zoos with wildlife of the Great Lakes region on display can also be worthwhile educational experiences. And there's no substitute for firsthand field study. You've found tracks, now you know what animals to look for. Read my notes on diet, put some bait out, sit quietly downwind with binoculars for a few hours, and see what comes along. Or follow the tracks a while. Use your imagination and common sense, and you'll be amazed at how much you can learn, and how rewarding the experiences can be.

As you use this book, remember that track identification is an inexact science. The illustrations in this book represent average *adult* tracks on *ideal* surfaces. But many of the tracks you encounter in the wild will be those of smaller-than-average animals, particularly in late spring and early summer. There are also larger-than-average animals, and injured or deformed ones, and animals that act unpredictably. Some creatures walk sideways on occasion. Most vary their gait so that in a single set of tracks front prints may fall ahead, behind, or beneath the rear. In addition, ground conditions are usually less than ideal in the wild, and animals often dislodge debris, which may further confuse the picture. Use this book as a guide, but anticipate lots of variations.

In attempting to identify tracks, remember that their size can vary greatly depending on the type of ground surface—sand that is loose or firm, wet or dry; a thin layer of mud over hard earth; deep soft mud; various lightly frozen surfaces; firm or loose dirt; dry or moist snow; a dusting of snow or frost over various surfaces; and so on. Note the surface from which the illustrations are taken and interpret what you find in nature accordingly.

You should also be aware that droplets from trees, windblown debris, and the like often leave a variety of marks on the ground that could be mistaken for animal tracks. While studying tracks, look around for and be aware of non-animal factors that might have left "tracks" of their own.

The range notes pertain only to the Great Lakes states of Illinois, Indiana, Michigan, Minnesota, New York, Pennsylvania, Ohio, and Wisconsin. Many trackmakers in this book also live elsewhere in North America. Range and habitat remarks are general guidelines because both are subject to change, from variations in both animal and human populations, climatic factors, pollution levels, acts of God, and so forth.

The size, height, and weight listed for each animal are those for average adults. Size refers to length from nose to tip of tail; height, the distance from ground to shoulder.

A few well-known species have been left out of this book: moles and bats, for example, which leave no tracks. Animals that may be common elsewhere but are rare, or occur only in the margins of the Great Lakes region, have also been omitted. Some species herein, particularly small rodents and birds, stand as representatives of groups of related species. In such cases the featured species is the one most commonly encountered and widely distributed. Related species, often with similar tracks, are listed in the notes. Where their tracks can be distinguished, guidelines for doing so are provided.

If you encounter an injured animal or an apparently orphaned infant, you may be tempted to take it home and care for it. Do not do so. Instead, report the animal to local authorities, who are better able to care for it. In addition, federal and state laws often strictly control the handling of wild animals. This is always the case with species classi-fied as *rare* or *endangered*. Animals are better left in the wild, and to do otherwise may be illegal.

TRACKING TIPS

At times you'll be lucky enough to find a perfectly clear and precise track that gives you all the information you need to identify the maker with a quick glance through this book. More often the track will be imperfect or fragmented. Following the tracks may lead you to a more readily identifiable print. Or maybe you have the time and inclination to follow an animal whose identity you already know in order to learn more about its habits, characteristics, and behavior.

Here are some tips for improving your tracking skills:

1. If you don't see tracks, look for disturbances—leaves or twigs in unnatural positions, debris or stones that appear to have been moved or turned. Stones become bleached on top over time, so a stone with its darker side up or sideways has recently been dislodged.

2. Push small sticks into the ground to mark individual signs. These will help you keep your bearings and "map out" the animal's general direction of travel.

3. Check immovable objects like trees, logs, and boulders along the route of travel for scratches, scuff marks, or fragments of hair.

4. Look at the ground from different angles, from standing height, from kneeling height and, if possible, from an elevated position in a tree or on a boulder or rise.

5. On very firm surfaces, place your cheek on the ground and ob-serve the surface, first through one eye, then the other, looking for unnatural depressions or disturbances.

6. Study the trail from as many different directions as possible. Trail signs may become obvious as the angle of light between them and your eyes changes, especially if dew, dust, or rain covers some parts of the ground surface.

7. Check for tracks beneath recently disturbed leaves or fallen debris.

8. Try not to focus your attention so narrowly that you lose sight of

the larger patterns of the country around you.

9. Keep your bearings. Some animals circle back if they become aware of being followed. If you find yourself following signs in a circular path, try waiting motionless and silent for a while, observing behind you.

10. Look ahead as far as possible as you follow signs. Animals take the paths of least resistance, so look for trails or runways. You may even catch sight of your quarry.

11. Animals are habitual in their movements between burrows, den sites, sources of water and food, temporary shelters, prominent trees, and so on. As you track and look ahead, try to anticipate where the creature might be going.

12. Stalk as you track; move as carefully and quietly as possible.

The secrets to successful tracking are patience and knowledge. Whenever you see an animal leaving tracks, go look at them and note the activity you observed. When you find and identify tracks, make little sketches alongside the book's illustrations, showing cluster patterns, or individual impressions that are different from those drawn. Make notes about what you learn in the wilds and from other readings. Eventually, you will build a body of knowledge from your own experience, and your future attempts at track identification will become easier and more certain.

This book is largely a compilation of the author's personal experiences. Your experiences with certain animals and their tracks may be identical, similar, or quite different. If you notice a discrepancy or find tracks that are not included in this book, carefully note your observations, or even amend the illustrations or text to reflect your own experiences. This book is intended for use in the field as a tool for identifying animal tracks of the Great Lakes region.

Mammals
Turtles
Amphibians

DEER MOUSE   *Peromyscus maniculatus*

Order: Rodentia (gnawing mammals). **Family:** Cricetidae (New World rats and mice). **Range and habitat:** throughout all Great Lakes states; in woods, rocks, grasslands, and nearly all other dry-land areas. **Size and weight:** 8 inches; 1 ounce. **Diet:** omnivorous, primarily seeds but also mushrooms and other fungi, berries, herbs, insects, larvae, and carrion. **Sounds:** occasional faint chirps, squeaks and chattering.

The abundant, wide-ranging, and familiar deer mouse is a medium-sized long-tailed mouse with pretty white underside, feet, pointy nose, and fairly large ears. Though primarily a mouse of the wilds, it is occasionally found in both abandoned and occupied buildings as well. A good climber, the deer mouse is active year round, generally nocturnal, and adaptable to many habitats. It makes up the main diet of many carnivorous birds and mammals, but is not so completely defenseless, as you might think. . . it may bite if handled carelessly.

The deer mouse usually leaves a distinctive track pattern—four-print clusters about 1.5 inches wide, walking or leaping up to 9 inches, with the tail dragging occasionally. As with any creature so small, its tracks are distinct only on rare occasions when surface conditions are perfect. More often you find merely clusters of tiny dimples in the mud or snow.

Tracks like these could also be made by eastern or western harvest mice, northern grasshopper mice (along the western edge of the region), or golden mice (in southern Illinois). Give or take an inch and a few fractions of an ounce, they're all quite similar. Mouse tracks, however, can be distinguished from those of voles and shrews, whose feet are about the same size: mouse track clusters are wider; voles and shrews tend to scuttle along or burrow under foliage or snow, rather than walk and hop about the surface, like mice. If you follow mouse tracks, more often than not they will lead to evidence of seed eating; shrews are strictly carnivorous.

Deer Mouse
life size in mud

SOUTHERN RED-BACKED VOLE   *Clethrionomys gapperi*
Boreal vole, gapper redback vole, red-backed mouse

Order: Rodentia (gnawing mammals). **Family:** Cricetidae (New World mice and rats). **Range and habitat:** Minnesota, northern Wisconsin and Michigan, western New York and Pennsylvania; in cool, damp forests and swampy fringe areas. **Size and weight:** 6 inches; 1 ounce. **Diet:** primarily vegetarian, including berries, herbs, nuts, seeds, lichens, and fungi; occasionally insects. **Sounds:** rarely audible to humans.

Voles, out and about by day, can frequently be glimpsed scurrying around. Though mouselike in habits, voles are squatter and plumper than mice, with no obvious neck and a slightly shorter and bushier tail. They are active year round, day and night, and are good climbers. Of all the voles present within the Great Lakes states, the southern red-backed vole is the only one with an easily distinguishable characteristic, its reddish back.

Several voles and volelike animals in the region, including meadow, prairie and pine voles, occupy ranges that overlap that of the red-backed vole and so closely resemble it (and one another) that positive identification of the animals, or their tracks, is difficult in the field.

Vole tracks are generally distinctive as a group because vole feet are peculiarly shaped and voles tend to walk and sit rather than run and leap like mice. Southern red-backed voles usually travel on the surface, while meadow voles generally live in denser vegetation and burrow along intricate systems of runways, which they often carefully line with cuttings of grass. Then again, Southern red-backed voles occasionally do that also. Walking pairs of red-backed vole tracks will be only an inch or so apart, with no tail marks. Other vole tracks are more mouselike, with 2 to 4 print clusters about 3 to 6 inches apart. Meadow voles have slightly longer tails, which may leave drag marks occasionally.

Southern Red-backed Vole
life size in mud

SHORT-TAILED SHREW

Sorex obscurus

Order: Insectivora (insect-eating mammals, including shrews, moles, and bats). **Family:** Soricidae (shrews). **Range and habitat:** throughout the Great Lakes region; in forests, grasslands, brushy or marshy areas; very adaptable, may turn up anywhere. **Size and weight:** 5 inches; 1 ounce. **Diet:** slugs, snails, spiders, insects, and larvae; occasionally mice and carrion. **Sounds:** commonly silent.

Shrews are vole-shaped creatures, but with shorter legs, a slightly more elongated body, and a long pointed snout. Shrew dentists have a big advantage in distinguishing the various species, because variations in unicuspid teeth are all that differentiate many of them. *All* shrews are little eating machines, though, with extremely high metabolism, evidenced by heartbeat and respiration rates around 1200 per minute. In fact, shrews consume more than their own body weight in food on a daily basis.

The shrews' constant and aggressive quest for food makes their tracks, in general, fairly easy to identify. The animals move around with more single-minded purpose than mice or voles, usually in a series of short hops in which the rear feet fall over the tracks of the front feet; the tails often drag, leaving the distinctive pattern shown, usually less than an inch in width. When individual impressions are more distinct, you may notice that shrews have five toes on both fore- and hind feet (most micelike creatures have four toes on the forefeet).

Nine shrew species live around the Great Lakes, all with similar habits and track patterns. Shrew dentists have a big advantage in distinguishing the various species because differences in unicuspid teeth are all that differentiate many of them.

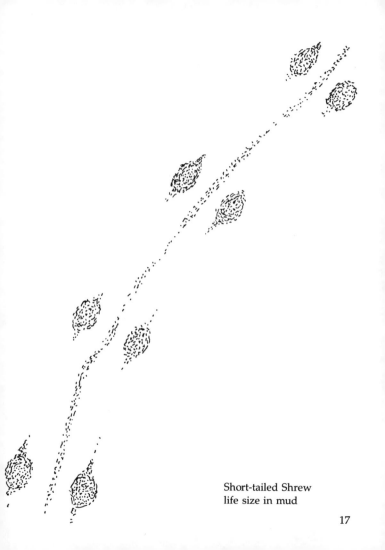

Short-tailed Shrew
life size in mud

PLAINS POCKET GOPHER
Thomomys bursarius

Order: Rodentia (gnawing mammals). **Family:** Geomyidae (pocket gophers). **Range and habitat:** Minnesota, western portions of Wisconsin, Ilinois and Indiana; fields, pastures, grasslands, and roadsides. **Size and weight:** 9 inches; 6 ounces. **Diet:** various foliage, twigs, bark, roots and tubors. **Sounds:** silent.

Pocket gophers are peculiar, highly evolved burrowing rodents named for the fur-lined cheek pockets in which they carry both food and nesting materials; the pockets can be turned inside out to empty their contents and for cleaning.

Plains pocket gophers look like small buff to grayish rats except that their large, yellowish front teeth are always showing; their lips close behind the teeth, so the animals can gnaw through earth and roots during tunneling without getting dirt in their mouths. Pocket gophers spend most of their lives in extensive tunnel systems. Pocket gophers living in snowy areas spend winter above ground, tunneling in the snow. In spring they clean out their underground tunnel systems, pushing accumulated soil into the snow tunnels. When the snow melts, meandering cores of this packed soil thus mark the courses of the winter tunnels. Other signs of pocket-gopher activity include tracks or tooth marks on limbs near their tunnel entrances, and plugged earthen mounds near those entrances.

The tracks are similar in size to those of a chipmunk, but the pocket gopher's elongated heel pads leave larger impressions. The most distinctive characteristic of pocket-gopher tracks, however, is the imprint of five toes on both front and rear feet; the relatively long digging claws on its front feet leave prominent marks, and the distance between the toe and the claw marks is greater than with any other similar-sized creature.

Plains Pocket Gopher
life size in mud

MEADOW JUMPING MOUSE   *Zapus hudsonius*

Order: Rodentia (gnawing mammals). **Family:** Zapodidae (jumping mice). **Range and habitat:** throughout the Great Lakes region; in low, lush grassy areas near water, but adaptable and may be found nearly anywhere. **Size and weight:** 9 inches; 1 ounce. **Diet:** vegetarian, including grasses, seeds, berries, and fungi. **Sounds:** frequent chirps at night between members of foraging groups.

The meadow jumping mouse varies in color from pale buff to rust, with a very long tail and relatively large, strong hind legs and feet. It is not easy to sight in the wild because it is generally nocturnal during warm weather and hibernates during the winter. You are most likely to see this little animal crossing the road in the beam of your car headlights.

The tracks of this jumping mouse are quite distinctive and should be easy to identify, even if the imprints are not very clear, because it is the only mouse living in the habitat described above that takes single jumps, or several in a series, of 6 inches to 5 feet each. Rear-foot impressions will be noticeably longer (around half an inch) than those of other similar-sized creatures, and its long tail leaves marks more frequently (either among the footprints or out to the side). But when leaping in a series of bounds, only the hind feet contact the ground, leaving a trail of small, widely spaced print-pairs without tail drag marks, also unique.

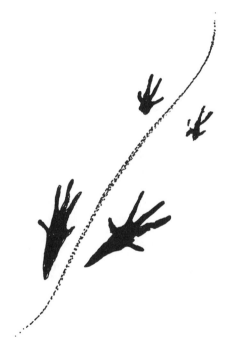

Meadow Jumping Mouse
life size in mud

EASTERN CHIPMUNK   *Tamias striatus*

Order: Rodentia (gnawing mammals). **Family:** Sciuridae (squirrels). **Range and habitat:** throughout Great Lakes region; in deciduous forests and fringe areas, also common in parks and camping areas. **Size and weight:** 9 inches; 3 ounces. **Diet:** vegetation, berries, grains and seeds, insects, carrion. **Sounds:** shrill and persistent "chip, chip."

The eastern chipmunk is the most widespread chipmunk species in the Great Lakes region, with one white stripe on each side. Least chipmunks, which also occur in forests in norther Minnesota and Wisconsin, have 2 white stripes on each side and are an inch or 2 shorter. Both chipmunks chatter nearly constantly, leaping and scurrying over the ground and up and down tree trunks during the daylight hours.

The track clusters of both chipmunks are usually 2 to 2.5 inches in width, with 7 to 15 inches between groups of prints. Chipmunks often run up on their toes, so rear-heel impressions may not show at all or may be less clear. The hind-foot tracks (five-toed) almost always fall in front of the forefoot tracks (four-toed), typical of all squirrel-family members.

If you find tracks like those described above in midwinter, however, you can assume they were left by a small squirrel rather than a chipmunk, because chipmunks tend to hole up with food caches in winter. At any rate, if you are indeed looking down at chipmunk tracks, regardless of season, you will probably catch sight of the maker, because chipmunks are noisy and not all that timid, particularly around areas frequented by people; in fact, they will more than likely approach you for a handout.

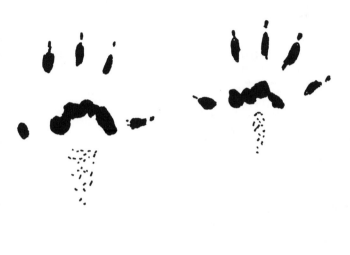

Eastern Chipmunk
life size in mud

THIRTEEN-LINED GROUND SQUIRREL
Striped gopher

Spermophilus tridecemlineatus

Order: Rodentia (gnawing mammals). **Family:** Sciuridae (squirrels). **Range and habitat:** absent from New York, Pennsylvania, and southern portions of Ilinois, Indiana, and Ohio; in shortgrass prairies, pastures, lawns, cemeteries and golf courses. **Size and weight:** 9 inches; 8 oz. **Diet:** omnivorous including herbs, seeds, fruits, insects, eggs, carrion. **Sounds:** variety of shrill and rapid chirps and bird-like whistles to signal alarm.

The two species of ground squirrels inhabiting the Great Lakes states vary greatly in appearance, but they are both *terrestrial*, living in extensive burrow systems. They tend to stand up and whistle when alarmed, rather than chattering like their arboreal cousins, and they never venture far from their burrow entrances. Thirteen-lined ground squirrels are solitary, slender, pale gray animals with prominent stripes or rows of spots on their sides. Franklin ground squirrels are much larger and darker, with no markings. Found only in western portions of Minnesota, Wisconsin, Illinois, and Indiana in fairly tall grass around the edges of fields and wooded areas, they live in colonies. Both species hibernate through at least six months of the year.

Thirteen-lined ground squirrel tracks are quite similar to chipmunk tracks in both size and shape, but are not found in wooded areas, where chipmunks live. Franklin ground squirrels leave larger tracks, but again, always near excavated ground burrows. Nine to 18 inches separate clusters of four prints made by running ground squirrels (these frenetic little animals rarely walk at all).

Another key feature of ground squirrel tracks is the toe prints. Ground squirrel toes, adapted for digging, tend to leave splayed prints. Their claws, being straighter and longer than those of chipmunks or tree squirrels, also an adaptation for digging, often leave imprints farther from the toes. One last difference: ground squirrels almost never leave tracks in snow; they are too busy sleeping away the winter.

13-lined Ground Squirrel
life size in mud

LEAST WEASEL   *Mustela nivalis*

Order: Carnivora (flesh-eating mammals). **Family:** Mustelidae (weasels and skunks). **Range and habitat:** absent only from western New York; in grassy and brushy fields, meadows, and swampy fringe areas. **Size and weight:** 7 inches overall; 2 ounces. **Diet:** almost exclusively mice, other small amphibians, baby rabbits and the like when available. **Sounds:** capable of wide range of hisses, chatters, and screams typical of all small weasels.

The least weasel, the smallest carnivore in North America, is easy to recognize in the field because it is distinctly smaller than either of its two cousins, the short- and long-tailed weasel. It has an almost nonexistent tail, compared to 3 or 4 inches of tail in its larger relatives. In winter, at least in northern parts of its range, the least weasel turns *entirely* white, without the black tail tip that characterizes both the short- and long-tailed weasels.

Least weasels demonstrate typical weasel behavior: most of their lives outside their dens are devoted to an energetic search for food that takes them far from home, mostly at night, occasionally up trees and into water, under downed trees, over logs, often backtracking and looping around wherever curiosity leads them to investigate.

These wandering hunting habits provide an excellent clue to differentiating the tracks of the small weasels from other similar-sized animals, particularly on snow, where you will have a much easier time following the trail. Weasels also often dive into the snow and reappear a few yards later, another unique behavior. Read the remarks on the short- and long-tailed weasels for other clues to recognizing weasel tracks.

Happily, least weasel tracks can usually be differentiated from those of its larger cousins by dimensions: 1.5-inch straddle and leaps no longer than 24 inches.

Least Weasel
life size in mud

AMERICAN TOAD   *Bufo americanus*

Order: Salientia (frogs, toads, and allies). **Family:** Bufonidae (true toads). **Range and habitat:** throughout the Great Lakes region; in moist woodlands and adjoining areas, wherever insects are abundant, usually but not necessarily within a mile of permanent dampness. **Size and weight:** 4 inches; 2 ounces. **Diet:** insects. **Sounds:** high-pitched musical trills.

Toads are small, froglike animals with dry, warty skin, in a variety of reddish, brown, and gray colors. They are primarily nocturnal, but can be seen at dawn or dusk, or even by day, crouching in a little niche, waiting for bugs.

Unlike frogs, toads often travel fairly far from sources of water. They do require water for breeding, however; look for their long, ropy strings of eggs in stagnant pond water.

Individual toad tracks can be confusing and might be mistaken for the tiny dimples and scratchings of tracks left by small mice or insects. A toad tends to sit quietly waiting for insects to fly past it, at which time it takes a few leaps in the direction of the wing noise, snares the bug with its long, sticky tongue, then repeats the procedure. Thus it may change direction of travel abruptly and often, commonly backtracking over earlier prints, which makes a very confusing picture on the ground.

Toad tracks generally consist of nothing more distinct than a trail of little holes and scrapes, with impressions that sometimes resemble little toad hands. The distinguishing characteristics are the mode of wandering, the short rows of four or five round dimples left by the toes of the larger rear feet, and the drag marks often left by the feet as the toad moves forward; those toe-drag marks point in the direction of travel.

You won't get warts from handling toads, but make sure you don't have insect repellent or other caustic substances on your hands that might injure the toads' sensitive skin.

American Toad
life size in mud

29

RED SQUIRREL   *Tamiasciurus hudsonicus*

Order: Rodentia (gnawing mammals). **Family:** Sciuridae (squirrels). **Range and habitat:** absent only from portions of Illinois and Ohio; in coniferous or mixed forests and occasionally nearby in swamp fringes. **Size and weight:** 12 inches; 8 ounces. **Diet:** nuts, fungi, insects, larvae, cones, seeds, and vegetation. **Sounds:** a great variety of noisy, ratchetlike sounds.

The red squirrel is active during the day year round. You often hear one scolding from a low branch before you see the little squirrel. Quite common throughout most of its range, this small, noisy squirrel is easy to identify by its rust or grayish-red coat of fur, fluffy rust-colored tail, and the white rings around its eyes. It lives in ground burrows as well as in downed logs and standing trees and is particularly fond of pine cones, which it shucks for the seeds, leaving piles of cone remnants everywhere. Occasionally in the fall, you may be startled by green cones falling systematically and seemingly unaided from tall coniferous trees. The red squirrel is up there, out of sight, cutting the cones; later it will gather them from the forest floor and hide them away for the cold months to come.

The red squirrel has long, curved toenails that act as hooks for tree climbing and which often leave definite imprints. Clear tracks show the squirrel's four toes on its front feet, and the five toes on its hind feet, which usually fall ahead of the front. Often the heel marks will be absent because the red squirrel is usually running quickly and nervously when it is on the ground; the track spacing may vary widely, with leaps from 8 to 30 inches. Individual prints may be as long as 1.5 inches.

Red Squirrel
life size in mud

SHORT-TAILED WEASEL
LONG-TAILED WEASEL

Mustela erminea
Mustela frenata

Order: Carnivora (flesh-eating mammals). **Family:** Mustelidae (the weasel family). **Range and habitat:** *M. frenata* occurs throughout the Great Lakes region; *M. erminia* is found in Minnesota, northern Wisconsin and Michigan, and western New York and Pennsylvania; both weasels frequent most habitats where water is nearby. **Size and weight:** variable, generally averages 12–14 inches; 6–10 ounces. **Diet:** small rodents, chipmunks, birds, amphibians. **Sounds:** may shriek or squeal when alarmed or making a kill, also purrs, chatters, hisses.

The short-tailed weasel is an inquisitive and aggressive little carnivore with a thin, elongated body and short, bushy tail. Brown with a white underside and feet during the summer months, in winter the weasel turns almost entirely white, save for the tip of its tail, which remains black. In this fur the short-tailed weasel is commonly known as an ermine.

The long-tailed weasel is a slightly larger and longer-tailed version of the short-tailed weasel. It, too, is an aggressive hunter by day and night, will climb and swim but generally confines its activities to an agile pursuit of prey on the ground, where it also finds various burrows, and it, too, grows a white coat with black tail tip in winter.

Short-tailed and long-tailed weasel tracks are impossible to distinguish conclusively. Generally, short-tailed track clusters are about 2 inches wide and less than 3 feet apart, whereas long-tailed weasel clusters may be as much as 3 inches in width, with leaps of up to 50 inches. But how do you really know whether the tracks were made by a large short-tailed weasel or a small long-tailed weasel?

If close study doesn't reveal fifth toe prints, individual weasel tracks can be tough to distinguish from those of squirrels or rabbits. But weasels usually *alternate* long and short bounds, and leave lines of doubled-over tracks with occasional tail-drag marks, whereas rabbits and squirrels tend to leave four separate prints in each cluster without tail drags. The latter also leave evidence of vegetarian diets, whereas weasels, being carnivores, do not.

Long-tailed Weasel
life size in mud

33

NORTHERN FLYING SQUIRREL
SOUTHERN FLYING SQUIRREL

Glaucomys sabrinus
Glaucomys volans

Order: Rodentia (gnawing mammals). **Family:** Sciuridae (squirrels). Range and habitat: *G. sabrinus* lives generally north of Lake Erie; *G. volans* is absent only from northern Minnesota and Wisconsin; in upland coniferous and occasionally mixed forests. **Size and weight:** 9–11 inches; 3–5 ounces. **Diet:** bark, fungi, lichen, seeds, insects, eggs, carrion. **Sounds:** generally silent but occasionally makes chirpy, bird-like noises.

Give or take an inch or two and a couple of ounces, the northern and southern flying squirrels are, for all practical purposes, indistinguishable, but since all flying squirrels are nocturnal, all you will likely see of either species is its tracks. That is, unless you happen to knock against or cut down one of the hollow trees in which both species are fond of nesting; in that case, if the squirrel that runs out is *small* and medium grayish, brown, it's likely you've had a rare glimpse of a flying squirrel.

During summer, flying squirrels don't leave much evidence of their passage. They live mostly in trees, using the fur-covered membrane that extends along each side of the body from the front to the rear legs to glide between trees and occasionally from tree to earth, where they usually leave no marks on the ground cover of their forest habitat. On snow, however, their tracks can be identified because they lead away from what looks like a miniature, scuffed snow-angel, the pattern left when a flying squirrel lands at the end of an aerial descent. The tracks may wander around a bit if the squirrel has foraged for morsels, but they will lead back to the trunk of a nearby tree before long.

Northern Flying Squirrel
life size in snow

MINK   *Mustela vison*

Order: Carnivora (flesh-eating mammals). **Family:** Mustelidae (the weasel family). **Range:** throughout Great Lakes region; in brushy or open forested areas along streams, lakes, and other wetlands. **Size and weight:** 24 inches; 3 pounds. **Diet:** primarily muskrats and smaller mammals; also birds, frogs, fish, crayfish, and eggs. **Sounds:** snarls, squeals, and hisses.

About the size of a small cat and medium brown all over, the mink is an excellent swimmer and may wander several miles a day searching for food along stream- and riverbanks and around the shorelines of lakes. Its den, too, is usually in a stream- or riverbank, an abandoned muskrat nest, or otherwise near water. Generally a nocturnal hunter, its tracks are likely to be the only indication you will have of its presence.

Intermediate in size between a long-tailed weasel and marten, the mink leaves either groups of four tracks like those illustrated or the characteristic double pair of tracks, usually not more than 26 inches apart. The tracks nearly always run along the edge of water. Though it has five toes both front and rear, it is quite common for only four toed imprints to be apparent. Like all mustelids, the mink employs its scent glands to mark territory; so, as you track it through its hunting ranges, you may notice a strong scent here and there, different but as potent as that of its relative the skunk. You might also, in snow, find signs of prey being dragged, invariably leading to the animal's den.

Mink
life size in mud

EASTERN SPOTTED SKUNK
Civet cat, hydrophobia cat

Spilogale putorius

Order: Carnivora (flesh-eating mammals). **Family:** Mustelidae (the weasel family). **Range and habitat:** Minnesota, parts of Wisconsin and Illinois, southern Indiana and Ohio; in brushy or sparsely wooded areas along streams, among boulders, and in prairies. **Size and weight:** 25 inches; 3 pounds. **Diet:** omnivorous, including rats, mice, birds, insects, eggs, carrion, seeds, fruit, and occasionally vegetation. **Sounds:** usually silent.

The spotted skunks are the smallest and most visually interesting of the North American skunks. About the size of a small housecat, with an assortment of white spots and streaks over its black coat, the spotted skunk has finer, silkier fur than the other skunks, is quicker and more agile, and occasionally climbs trees, although it doen't stay aloft for long. Like all skunks, it is primarily nocturnal, but you might see it at dawn or dusk, or foraging during the daylight in winter, when hunger keeps it active. Skunks have the most highly effective scent glands of all the mustelids and can, when severely provoked, shoot a fine spray of extremely irritating methyl mercaptan as far as 25 feet.

Skunk tracks are all similar, with five toes on each foot leaving prints, toenail prints commonly visible, and front tracks slightly less flat-footed than rear. Only size and irregular stride may help distinguish the tracks of the spotted skunk from those of the twice-as-large striped skunk, which is widespread and common throughout the Great Lakes states. Spotted skunk tracks will be about 1.25 inches long at most; adult striped skunks leave tracks up to 2 inches in length. On the other hand, the quick spotted skunk leaves a foot or more between *clusters* of prints when running, while the larger striped skunk lopes along with only about 5 or 6 inches between more strung-out track groups.

Because skunks can hold most land animals at bay with their formidable scent, owls are their chief predators. If you are following a skunk trail that ends suddenly, perhaps a bit of black and white fur remaining mysteriously where the tracks disappear, you might be able to guess what transpired.

Eastern Spotted Skunk
life size in mud

MUSKRAT

Ondatra zibethicus

Order: Rodentia (gnawing mammals). **Family:** Cricetidae (New World rats and mice). **Range and habitat:** throughout Great Lakes region; in streams, lakes, ponds, and marshes. **Size and weight:** 24 inches; 4 pounds. **Diet:** aquatic vegetation; occasionally shellfish and small aquatic animals. **Sounds:** high-pitched squeaks.

The muskrat is a large brown rat with a volelike appearance, modified for its aquatic life by a rudderlike scaly tail and partially webbed hind feet. Muskrats associate readily with beavers and occasionally nest within the superstructure of beaver lodges. More often, muskrats burrow into riverbanks or construct lodges similar to those of beavers but extending only a couple of feet above water level and composed of aquatic vegetation, primarily grasses and reeds, rather than trees. Muskrat lodges always have underwater entrances. Mainly nocturnal, the muskrat can be seen during the late afternoon or at dusk, pulling the V of its ripples across a still water surface, tail skulling behind, mouth full of grass for supper or nest-building.

Muskrat tracks are nearly always found in mud close to water. The muskrat is one of the few rodents with five toes on its front feet, but its truncated inner toes often leave no imprint. It leaves tracks about 2 inches apart when walking to 12 inches apart when running, with the tail sometimes dragging as well. The track of the hind foot is usually more distinctive than that of the front, and the stiff webbing of hair between the toes is often visible.

Muskrat
life size in mud

EASTERN GRAY SQUIRREL   *Sciurus carolinensis*

Order: Rodentia (gnawing mammals). **Family:** Sciuridae (squirrels). **Range and habitat:** throughout Great Lakes region; in hardwood (especially oak) or mixed hardwood-evergreen forests, and occasionally nearby in swamp fringes. **Size and weight:** 20 inches; 1 pound. **Diet:** mostly acorns and cone seeds, also various nuts, fungi, insects and larvae, some vegetation. **Sounds:** variety of rapid, raspy barks.

The large eastern gray squirrel is such a common park animal that most of us are familiar with it. It is normally gray above, with an off-white belly and long bushy tail. (In some parts of its range, a black phase is locally common.) Active all day, year round, the eastern gray squirrel nests in tree cavities or in conspicuous nests made of sticks and shredded bark, usually 20 feet or more above the ground, but spends a lot of time on the ground searching for nuts and seeds and ranges widely around its home trees.

Because of their wandering habits, eastern gray squirrels leave a lot of tracks in areas traveled by other similar-sized animals, and partial track impressions can be confusing. Gray squirrels are often running, so their long rear heels don't leave prints. The real keys to recognizing gray squirrel tracks are the number of toes—four on the front feet and five on the rear—and the track characteristics common to all members of the squirrel family: front tracks close together; and the two middle toes of the front feet and three middle toes of the rear feet, almost always close together and lined up ahead of each heel print, with only the outer toes splayed out to the sides. The toes are also relatively farther from the heel pads in squirrel tracks than in weasel-family tracks. If after careful investigation, combined as always with consideration of habitat and pattern of movement, you've determined tracks belong to a squirrel-family member, as opposed to a cottontail, for example, or one of the smaller weasels, then the size of the tracks will distinguish the gray squirrel: front tracks about an inch across; rear tracks less than 2.5 inches long, depending on surface condition and how much of the heel has left an impression; track straddle about 4.5 inches; leaps of 2 to 3 feet.

Eastern Gray Squirrel
life size in mud

43

FOX SQUIRREL   *Sciurus niger*

Order: Rodentia (gnawing mammals). **Family:** Sciuridae (squirrels). **Range and habitat:** absent only from portions of northern Wisconsin, the north peninsula of Michigan, and western New York; in open hardwood or mixed coniferous forests. **Size and weight:** 25 inches; 2 to 3 pounds. **Diet:** prefers hickory nuts and acorns, also variety of other nuts, seeds, fungi, berries, bird eggs, bark, buds. **Sounds:** ratchet-like, rapid and raspy barks.

The fox squirrel is the largest tree squirrel in America. It can be distinguished from the gray squirrel by color as well as size: the underside of the fox squirrel is generally more buff than white, and there is more rust and yellowish fur mixed with the gray of its coat, particularly on its tail.

It's very difficult, however, in practical terms, to distinguish between the tracks of the two, because while there is clearly a difference in body size between the two, all adult fox squirrels do not necessarily have larger feet than all adult gray squirrels.

A good clue to the identity of the track maker may be found in wandering and eating patterns rather than track measurements: gray squirrels tend to wander far from their home trees, searching for food, which they often eat where they find it; fox squirrels are more likely to carry edibles back to a favorite feeding perch. So if in following the tracks, you discover a large deposit of food remnants near a log, stump, or branch, the tracks are probably those of a fox squirrel. To be certain, however, you could hang around quietly for a while and see what activity you can observe.

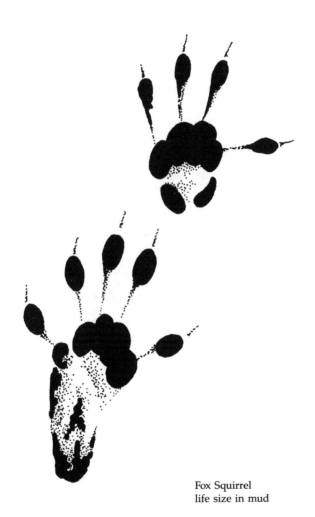

Fox Squirrel
life size in mud

STRIPED SKUNK

Mephitis mephitis

Order: Carnivora (flesh-eating mammals). **Family:** Mustelidae (weasels and skunks). **Range and habitat:** throughout Great Lakes region; in semi-open country, mixed woods, brushland, and open fields. **Size and weight:** 24 inches; 10 pounds. **Diet:** omnivorous, including mice, eggs, insects, grubs, fruit, carrion. **Sounds:** usually silent.

Often found dead along highways, this cat-sized skunk is easily recognized by the two broad stripes running the length of its back, meeting at head and shoulders to form a cap. A thin white stripe runs down its face. Active year round, it is chiefly nocturnal but may be sighted shortly after sunset or at dawn, snuffling around for food. It seeks shelter beneath buildings as well as in ground burrows or other protected den sites, and protects itself, when threatened, with a fine spray of extremely irritating methyl mercaptan; everyone knows what that smells like.

Striped skunk tracks are similar to but larger than those of the smaller spotted skunk, and its elongated heel pads are more often apparent because it's not as quick, agile, or high-strung as its smaller cousin. With five closely spaced toes and claws on all feet usually leaving marks, its tracks can't be mistaken for any others of its size; the spacing is distinctive, too: generally less than six inches between track groups, whether they consist of walking pairs or strung-out loping groups of four tracks.

Striped Skunk
life size in mud

BULLFROG

Rana catesbiana

Order: Salientia (frogs, toads, and allies). **Family:** Ranidae (true frogs). **Range and habitat:** widespread throughout most of the Great Lakes states; in ponds, lakes, marshes and swamps, year-around bodies of water. **Size and weight:** body 5–8 inches, with long legs; 4 ounces. **Diet:** insects. **Sounds:** low-pitched croaks, deep jug-o-rum, especially at dawn and dusk.

Eighty-one species of frogs live north of the Rio Grande River, of which the bullfrog is the largest. Varying in color from a mottled darker-gray to green, with an off-white belly, bullfrogs live in or very near water because they must keep their skin wet and they breed in water. They use distinctive vocalizations to signal each other and to attract mates. The 4-to-6-inch-long vegetarian tadpoles take up to two years to transform into carnivorous adults. As with all toads and frogs, be sure your hands are free of insect repellent or other caustic substances before you handle a bullfrog as it has particularly sensitive skin.

Frogs walk or hop in a more plantigrade manner than toads, so their tracks tend to be more easily recognizable. You will commonly find impressions of the full soles of their feet and might even be able to see that their hind feet are webbed, except the last joint of the longest toe, although these delicate membranes don't always imprint. The toed-in imprints of the small front feet combined with a straddle of 5 or 6 inches should leave no doubt about the identity of bullfrog tracks, even if the hind-foot impressions are less than distinct.

Other frog species living in the Great Lakes states include the northern leopard, green, wood, and pickerel frogs, whose tracks are similar to but smaller than those of the bullfrog. The adult northern leopard frog averages 3.5 inches in length; its tracks are nearly identical to those of the bullfrog in shape, but considerably smaller in foot size, width of straddle, length of stride and leaps, and depth of impression in soft surfaces.

Bullfrog
life size in mud

OPOSSUM   *Didelphis virginiana*

Order: Marsupialia (pouched mammals). **Family:** Didelphiidae.
Range and habitat: absent only from northern Minnesota, Wisconsin
and Michigan; in woodlands and adjoining areas, and farmlands,
generally remaining near streams and lakes; also common around
human habitations. **Size and weight:** 25 inches; 12 pounds. **Diet:** this
opportunistic omnivore prefers fruits, vegetables, insects, small
mammals, birds, eggs, carrion; also garbage and pet food. **Sounds:** a
gurgling hiss when annoyed.

The generally nocturnal opossum appears fairly ordinary: it looks
like a large, long-haired rat, with pointed nose, pale-gray fur, and a
long, scaly, reptilian tail. Primarily terrestrial, the opossum may nest
in an abandoned burrow or a fallen tree, but will climb to escape
danger. Other than climbing, its only defense mechanism is an
ability to feign death, or "play possum."

In many respects, however, the opossum is the most peculiar
animal residing on this continent. Among the oldest and most primi-
tive of all living mammals, it is the only animal in North America
with a prehensile (grasping) tail, the only nonprimate in the animal
kingdom with an opposable (thumblike) digit (the inside toes on the
hind feet), and the only marsupial on the continent. As many as 14
young are born prematurely after only 13 days of gestation, weighing
1/15 ounce each (the whole litter would fit into a teaspoon!). The tiny
babies crawl into their mother's pouch, where they remain for the
next two months. After emerging from the pouch, they often ride
around on the mother's back for some time. All of this is pretty un-
usual behavior.

Opossums leave easily identifiable tracks: the opposable hind
thumb usually points 90 degrees or more away from the direction of
travel, and the five front toes spread widely. Like raccoons, opossums leave tracks in a row of pairs. Each pair consists of one front-
and one rear-foot imprint, always close to or slightly overlapping
each other, and the pairs are from 5 to 11 inches apart, depending on
size and speed. The opossum's long tail frequently leaves drag marks
on soft surfaces.

Opossum
life size in mud

WOODCHUCK
Groundhog, marmot

Marmota monax

Order: Rodentia (gnawing mammals). **Family:** Sciuridae (squirrels). **Range and habitat:** throughout Great Lakes region; in open woods, meadows, fields, pastureland, also brushy, rocky ravines and along stream courses; a very adaptable animal. **Size and weight:** 22 inches; 8 pounds. **Diet:** almost any tender, succulent vegetation available. **Sounds:** loud, shrill chirps and whistles, especially when alarmed.

With a day set aside in February for us to concern ourselves with whether or not groundhogs see their shadows, these animals have become quite familiar. You may have seen the short-legged, plump, brown woodchuck alongside a highway, grazing and seemingly oblivious to passing traffic, or on the pavement, where its obliviousness has led it to Oblivion. Or you may have discovered one of its extensive burrows, with two or more entrances, in your lawn. The woodchuck, active during the day and hibernating during the winter, leads a solitary life but is not particularly shy of human activity.

In the absence of highway or lawn grass, woodchucks seem to like to wander along stream courses, seeking the succulent plants that flourish in such environs. On firm mud, you more than likely will find tracks like those on the right, with distinct claw and heel-pad impressions. On softer mud or wet spring snow, the tracks will look more like the two on the left. Because of their size and squirrel-family characteristics, you're not likely to mistake woodchuck tracks for anything else, but walking strides of about 3 inches and rare leaps of not more than 15 to 18 inches will verify the identity of this easygoing woodland creature.

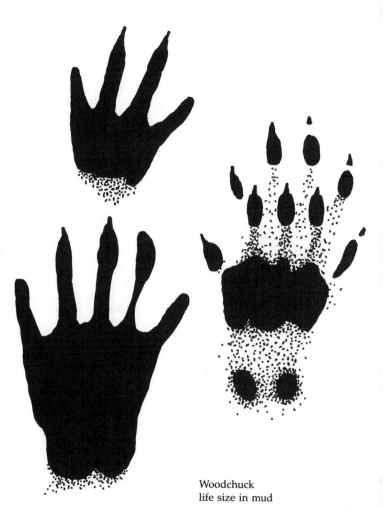

Woodchuck
life size in mud

53

MARTEN
Pine marten, American sable

Martes americana

Order: Carnivora (flesh-eating mammals). **Family:** Mustelidae (the weasel family). **Range and habitat:** parts of northern Minnesota and Wisconsin; in coniferous forests, occasionally in adjoining areas, including rock slides. **Size and weight:** 30 inches; 3 pounds. **Diet:** primarily red squirrels; also other small mammals, birds, eggs, berries, and nuts. **Sounds:** generally silent.

Between a mink and a fisher in size, the energetic and adaptable marten is typically weasel-shaped, buff-colored on its throat and brownish or rusty-brown over the rest of its body, with a long, fluffy tail. Solitary, generally nocturnal, and always extremely wary, it is seldom sighted in the wild, but it is also inquisitive and can be lured from its den with squeaking, mouselike noises made by kissing the back of your hand. The marten covers distances of many miles in a single night's hunting and is active year round. A skillful tree climber, it spends a lot of time off the ground and often dens in tree cavities; the marten can nearly always be found in forests the red squirrel inhabits.

The marten leaves few signs in the summer forest except for scat stations, spots where droppings are repeatedly left. On snow, its tracks are very similar to but slightly larger than mink tracks. Small, thin pads behind five toes and nails are normally visible in marten tracks, with size and spacing somewhat larger than that of the mink. Marten tracks, however, will tend to lead to and from trees and rarely venture near water, unlike the mink's. Walking tracks are usually 6 to 9 inches apart, running clusters 24 inches apart, and bounding pairs of overlapping prints as much as 40 inches apart.

Marten
life size in mud

BOBCAT
Wildcat, bay lynx

Felis rufus

Order: Carnivora (flesh-eating mammals). **Family:** Felidae (cats).
Range and habitat: in northern Minnesota, Wisconsin and Michigan;
western Illinois; southern Indiana; and western New York; in forests
and swamp fringes. **Size and weight:** 30 inches; 35 pounds. **Diet:**
small mammals and birds; rarely carrion. **Sounds:** less vocal than the
lynx, but capable of generic cat family range of noises.

Closely related to the lynx, the bobcat is a very adaptable feline,
afield both day and night and wandering as much as 50 miles in a day
of hunting, occasionally into suburban areas. It is primarily a ground
hunter, but will climb trees and drop onto unexpecting prey if the op-
portunity presents itself. You could mistake it for a large tabby cat
with a bobbed tail, but the similarity ends there, for the bobcat has
quite a wild disposition combined with much greater size, strength
and razor-sharp claws and teeth.

You can expect to encounter bobcat tracks almost anywhere. You'll
know the roundish tracks belong to a cat because the rectractile claws
never leave imprints and the toes usually spread a bit more than a
dog's. Bobcat tracks are too large to be mistaken for those of a
domestic cat, however. The animal's weight will have set the tracks
deeper in a soft surface than you would expect from a housecat, and
domestic cats have pads that are single-lobed at the front end. Bobcat
tracks are clearly smaller than those of a lynx and are therefore easily
identifiable by process of elimination.

Bobcat
life size in mud

GRAY FOX
RED FOX

Urocyon cinereoargenteus
Vulpes vulpes

Order: Carnivora (flesh-eating mammals). **Family:** Canidae (dogs). **Range and habitat:** throughout Great Lakes region; in open forests and brushy, sparsely wooded fields and meadows nearby. **Size and weight:** 40–42 inches; 12–15 pounds. **Diet:** omnivorous, including small mammals, birds, insects, eggs, fruit, nuts, grains, and other forage. **Sounds:** gray fox—normally silent; occasionally short barking yips; red fox—a variety of doglike noises.

The gray is generally more nocturnal and secretive than the red fox. The only canine in America with the ability to climb, it frequently seeks refuge and food in trees, but cottontails are the mainstay of its diet. It typically dens among boulders on the slopes of rocky ridges or in rock piles, hollow logs, or the like; unlike the red fox, it uses these dens in winter as well as summer.

The sleek little red fox usually leaves a distinctive, nearly straight line of tracks, the front track slightly wider than the rear. Its feet are quite furry, adapted to the generally higher elevations of its habitat; as a result the prints of pads and toes are often indistinct unless the surface is quite firm, in which case only a partial pad imprint will appear, making the toe prints clearly separate. The claws always leave marks, although in deep snow the tail may brush over and obscure some of the finer points of the tracks. Red fox tracks could be mistaken for those of a small domestic dog, except that the fox's heel pad has a unique curved bar and the heel pads of domestic dogs tend to be longer, extending forward between the outer toes. Also, a walking red fox leaves tracks from 12 to 18 inches apart, a somewhat longer stride than that of a similar-sized domestic dog.

Gray fox tracks are very similar to those of the red fox, except that the prints are usually more distinct due to the relative lack of fur on the animal's feet. The tracks always show the imprints of claws and may be the same size or slightly smaller and narrower than the red fox's, with 7 to 12 inches between walking prints.

Gray Fox
life size in mud

COYOTE
Brush wolf, prairie wolf

Canis latrans

Order: Carnivora (flesh-eating mammals). **Family:** Canidae (dogs). **Range and habitat:** throughout the Great Lakes states; primarily in prairies, open woodlands, and brushy fringes, but very adaptable; can turn up anywhere. **Size and weight:** 48 inches; 45 pounds. **Diet:** omnivorous, including rodents and other small mammals, fish, carrion, insects, berries, grains, nuts, and vegetation. **Sounds:** wide range of canine sounds; most often heard yelping in group chorus late at night.

An important controller of small rodents, the smart, adaptable coyote is—unlike the gray wolf—steadily expanding its range. About the size of a collie, the coyote is a good runner and swimmer and has great stamina. Despite its wide range, it is shy, and you will be lucky to see one in the wild.

Typically canine, the coyote's front paw is slightly larger than the rear, and the front toes tend to spread wider, though not as wide as the bobcat's. The toenails nearly always leave imprints. The shape of coyote pads is unique, the front pads differing markedly from the rear, as shown, and the outer toes are usually slightly larger than the inner toes on each foot. The coyote tends to walk in a straight line and keep its tail down, which often leaves an imprint in deep snow. These characteristics plus walking strides of 8 to 16 inches and leaps to 10 feet may help you distinguish coyote tracks from those of domestic dogs with feet of the same size.

Coyote
life size in mud

61

BADGER

Taxidea taxus

Order: Carnivora (flesh-eating mammals). **Family:** Mustelidae (the weasel family). **Range and habitat:** absent only from New York and Pennsylvania, and parts of southern Ohio, Indiana, and Illinois; in meadows, semiopen fields, grasslands, and prairies, wherever ground-dwelling rodents are abundant. **Size and weight:** 28 inches; 20 pounds. **Diet:** carnivorous, including all smaller rodents, snakes, birds, eggs, insects, and carrion. **Sounds:** may snarl or hiss when alarmed or annoyed.

The badger is a solitary creature that digs up most of its food and tunnels into the earth to escape danger. Its powerful short legs and long strong claws are well suited to its earth-moving ways, and badgers can reputedly dig faster than a man with a shovel. Above ground the badger is a fierce fighter threatened only by much larger carnivores. The animal is active in daylight and not too shy, even entering campgrounds in its search for food. Its facial markings are quite distinctive and easily recognized: the face is black with white ears and cheeks and a white stripe running from its nose over the top of its head. The rest of the body is light brown or gray, and the feet are black.

Badger tracks show five long, clear toe prints of each foot and obvious marks left by the long front claws. The animal walks on its soles, which may or may not leave complete prints. Its pigeon-toed trail may be confused with the porcupine's in deep snow, but a porcupine trail will invariably lead to a tree or into a natural den, a badger's to a burrow of its own excavation; another clue: the badger's short, soft tail rarely leaves a mark.

Badger
life size in mud

FISHER
Black cat

Martes pennanti

Order: Carnivora (flesh-eating mammals). **Family:** Mustelidae (the weasel family). **Range and habitat:** parts of northern Minnesota and Wisconsin; in coniferous and mixed forests and occasionally in cutover areas. **Size and weight:** 36 inches; 15 pounds. **Diet:** primarily smaller mammals, including porcupines; also insects, birds, eggs, fish, frogs, and, infrequently, fruit and vegetation. **Sounds:** hisses, growls, and snarls.

The fisher likes fish when it finds them washed ashore, but will not enter water to catch them. This dark brown weasel with its foot-long bushy, tapering tail is slightly larger than the marten, more adaptable in habitat, and wider ranging, covering a territory of 150 square miles or more. Very aggressive and strong for its size, the fisher is terrifically speedy whether on the ground or climbing, all of which may explain why it is among the few predators that kill and eat porcupines regularly. Its diet also includes other weasel-family relatives.

Because the fisher is fairly scarce and nocturnal, and prefers wild mature forests, you will be very lucky to sight one in its natural habitat, but it is active year round and its tracks are easy enough to recognize. Typical of the weasel clan, all five toes and claws usually leave imprints, as do the rather narrow pads. Fisher tracks generally lead to or away from trees and avoid water. Walking stride is 10 to 15 inches, with clusters of running tracks 3 to 4 feet apart and 4 to 6 feet between leaping pairs of overlapping prints in the common weasel mode.

Fisher
life size in mud

PORCUPINE
Porky, quill pig

Erethizon dorsatum

Order: Rodentia (gnawing mammals). **Family:** Erethizontidae (porcupines). **Range and habitat:** New York, northwest Pennsylvania, and northern Minnesota, Wisconsin, and Michigan; usually in forested areas, also in brushy fringes, fields, meadows, and semi-desert areas; a very adaptable animal. **Size and weight:** 30 inches; 25 pounds. **Diet:** vegetarian, including bark, leaves, fruits, berries, nuts, flowers. **Sounds:** normally quiet; capable of a great variety of grunts, whines, and harmonicalike noises and rapid teeth clicking.

The porcupine is one of the few animals whose tracks you can follow with reasonable expectation of catching up with their maker. Often out during daylight hours, it moves quite slowly if not alarmed, stops frequently to nibble at vegetation, and does not see well, so if you're quiet, you can usually observe this peaceable animal at your and its leisure. An alarmed porcupine climbs a tree to escape danger, only using its quills as a last-ditch defense against an outright attack; and the porcupine cannot fling its quills, so there's no danger to any creature with enough sense to stay out of direct contact, a requisite that regrettably excludes many domestic dogs.

Often the porcupine's distinctive shuffling gait and dragging whisk-broom tail may be the only clear track signs it leaves behind, especially in deep snow. In winter, porcupine trails often lead to or away from a large coniferous tree, where the animal both sleeps and dines on bark and needles; alternatively, it may hole up in a den beneath a stump or in another ground-level shelter. Occasionally a piece of snow or mud that has stuck to a porcupine's foot will dislodge intact, revealing the unique pebbled texture of its soles. Imprints from the long claws are also often visible.

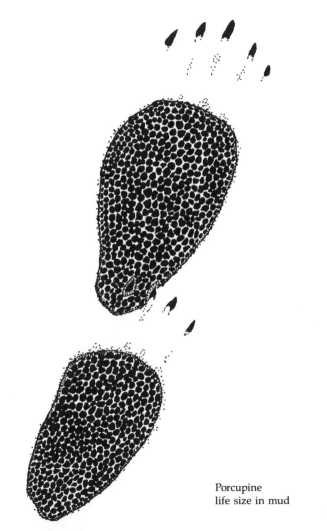

Porcupine
life size in mud

RACCOON
Coon

Procyon lotor

Order: Carnivora (flesh-eating mammals). **Family:** Procyonidae (raccoons, ringtails, and coatis). **Range and habitat:** throughout Great Lakes states; in forest fringe and rocky areas near streams, ponds, and lakes. **Size and weight:** 36 inches; 25 pounds. **Diet:** omnivorous, including fish, amphibians, shellfish, insects, birds, eggs, mice, carrion, berries, nuts, and vegetation. **Sounds:** a variety of shrill cries, whistles, churrs, growls, and screeches.

From childhood most of us know the raccoon by its mask of black fur and its black tail stripes on an otherwise grayish-brown body. It's familiar as a character in kids' books and frontier lore, frequently seen as a road kill, and is both curious and bold enough to be a fairly common visitor to campgrounds and even residential homes nearly everywhere within its range. Chiefly nocturnal, raccoons are more commonly sighted in suburban neighborhoods raiding garbage cans and terrorizing family hounds than in wildlands. Interesting and intelligent animals with manual dexterity of great renown, raccoons are also reputed to make lively and intriguing pets, provided they are closely supervised.

Raccoons like to wash or tear food items apart in water, which apparently improves their manual sensitivity. Much of their food comes from aquatic prospecting, so you will often find their tracks near water. When a raccoon walks, its left rear foot is placed next to the right front foot, and so forth, forming paired track clusters. On firm mud or dirt, you will likely find tracks like those on the right, with distinct print details. On softer mud or wet spring snow, the tracks will look more like the two on the left. Running-track clusters tend to be bunched irregularly. The walking stride of a raccoon is about 7 inches; leaps average 20 inches.

Raccoon
life size in mud

RIVER OTTER
Land otter

Lutra canadensis

Order: Carnivora (flesh-eating mammals). **Family:** Mustelidae (the weasel family). **Range and habitat:** throughout the Great Lakes states; in and near lakes and streams. **Size and weight:** 48 inches; 25 pounds. **Diet:** fish, amphibians, shellfish and other aquatic invertebrates, snakes, turtles, birds, eggs. **Sounds:** chirps, chatters, chuckles, grunts, and growls.

The river otter is a dark brown weasel about as large as a medium-sized dog, with a thick, hairless tail adapted for swimming, much like that of the muskrat; in fact, the river otter closely resembles the muskrat in appearance and habitat, but is much larger, strictly carnivorous, and quite a bit more animated. Both in and out of water, alone or in the company of others, the river otter seems to be a graceful and exuberant playful animal. Active during the daylight hours, the otter is wary of humans. Still, you might occasionally sight one in the wild; more commonly you may find, in summer, the flattened grass where otters have rolled, leaving their musky odor behind, or in winter, marks on snow or ice where they've playfully slid on their bellies.

River otter tracks are relatively easy to find and identify within the otter's range. The webs of the rear feet often leave distinct marks on soft surfaces, and claw marks usually are present. Individual tracks measure up to 3.5 inches across and due to their size cannot be confused with those of any other animal with similar aquatic habitat. River otters do venture into woodlands as well, however, where small otter tracks could be mistaken for those of a large fisher, but fisher tracks will lead to or from coniferous trees before long, in somewhat more linear patterns, while otter tracks meander, forming a trail roughly 8 to 10 inches wide and generally leading to or from water systems. Also, the river otter normally leaves groups of four tracks 13 to 30 inches apart, when it's not sliding on its belly.

River Otter
life size in mud

LYNX

Felis lynx

Order: Carnivora (flesh-eating mammals). **Family:** Felidae (cats). **Range and habitat:** northern Minnesota, Wisconsin, and Michigan; in forests, woodlands, and swamp fringes, wherever the snowshoe hare is found. **Size and weight:** 36 inches; 30 pounds. **Diet:** primarily snowshoe hares; occasionally other small mammals and birds. **Sounds:** quite vocal, including hisses, spitting noises, growls, caterwauls, and other generic cat family noises.

Closely related to the bobcat in both size and characteristics, the lynx has adapted to its generally more northerly range with longer legs, longer and denser fur, and larger, thickly furred paws that provide buoyancy in deep snow and make them excellent swimmers; conspicuous black ear tufts also distinguish it from the bobcat, whose range it does overlap. The lynx relies on snowshoe hares as its dietary mainstay, and its range precisely overlaps the wilder, more remote portions of the hare's range. When the cyclical hare population is at a peak, lynxes have larger litters, but when the hares are scarce, the cats bear fewer offspring. The lynx hunts on the ground, but will go into trees to catch prey or to wait for ground animals to pass beneath it.

The wary lynx is most active at night; by day, it tends to rest somewhere, venturing out only to kill unlucky prey that happens by, so you will seldom see it in the wild, but its tracks are unique, clearly larger than those of the bobcat. The range of the lynx also overlaps that of the mountain lion. Their feet are roughly the same size, but lynx trails are only about 7 or 8 inches wide, and its walking stride is around 12 inches. The lynx is also much lighter than the mountain lion, causing shallower tracks on yielding surfaces.

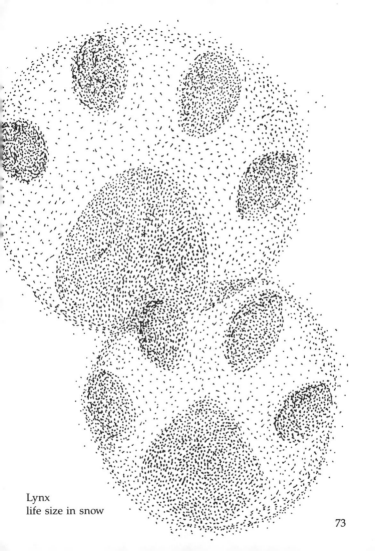

Lynx
life size in snow

WHITE-TAILED DEER
Odocoileus virginianus
Whitetail, Virginia deer

Order: Artiodactyla (even-toed hoofed mammals). **Family:** Cervidae (deer). **Range and habitat:** throughout Great Lakes region; in deciduous and mixed woodlands, nearby meadows, river bottomlands, creeksides, open brushy areas, and swamp fringes. **Height and weight:** 42 inches at shoulder; 250 pounds. **Diet:** browse from shrubs and lower tree limbs; less frequently fungi, nuts, grains, grasses, and herbs. **Sounds:** low bleats, guttural grunts, snorts, and whistles of alarm.

The white-tailed deer is recognizable by the all-white underside of its tail, which the animal raises prominently when it runs. It usually has a home range of only a square mile or so, although some migrate to swamps in cold weather. White-tailed deer usually gather in groups of no more than 3 animals, except in the dead of winter when the group may swell to 25. They spend their days browsing and quietly chewing their cud and when startled run only short distances to the nearest cover.

The white-tailed deer's range overlaps that of the moose, but its tracks are easy enough to identify. Individual tracks are relatively long and slender, averaging about 3 inches in length; the dewclaws will leave prints in snow or soft earth. Taken alone, a single track could be confused with one left by a young moose. When running, the white-tailed deer tends to trot, often leaving tracks in a more or less straight line, with up to 6 feet between track groups. Its walking gait is less than 20 inches, with tracks frequently doubled up, as the rear feet cover prints left by the front. Also, the white-tailed deer generally lives in open forests and upland meadows, whereas the moose prefers lowlands with lakes and ponds.

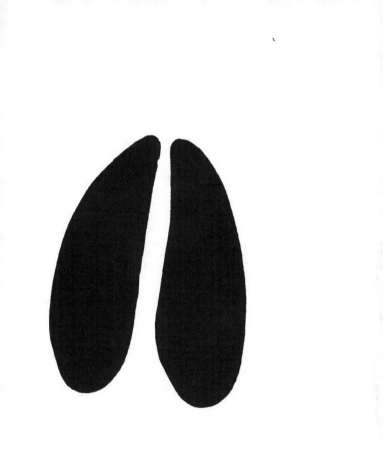

White-tailed Deer
life size in mud

GRAY WOLF
Timber wolf

Canis lupus

Order: Carnivora (flesh-eating mammals). **Family:** Canidae (dogs). **Range and habitat:** northern Minnesota, Wisconsin, and Michigan; in forested and open areas, to far above timberline. **Size and weight:** 72 inches; 110 pounds. **Diet:** primarily deer as well as smaller mammals down to mice; occasionally berries, birds, eggs, and insects. **Sounds:** variety of canine noises, including barks, snarls, and growls; occasionally various howls, solo or in chorus, often of lengthy duration.

You can consider yourself fortunate indeed if you sight a gray wolf in the wild these days, for they have been systematically exterminated from nearly all the contiguous 48 states. The gray wolf is rare and endangered within the Great Lakes region.

The gray wolf, an intelligent, gregarious animal that mates for life and has quite complicated social organizations, would seem to deserve protection from eradication. Gray wolves pose no threat to humans.

You may not see the wary wolf, but its tracks are out there to be found and identified in its remote habitats. Wolf tracks show the four toes and nails typical of the canine family, with the front foot slightly larger than the rear. Angularity of pads, inner toes slightly larger than outer, and overall dimensions distinguish wolf tracks; no other canine is likely to leave tracks 5 inches or more in length in remote wilderness areas, and no other canine covers ground like the gray wolf, with its walking stride of nearly 30 inches and leaps of 9 feet or more.

Gray Wolf
½ life size in mud

EASTERN COTTONTAIL   *Sylvilagus floridanus*

Order: Lagomorpha (rabbitlike mammals). **Family:** Leporidae (hares and rabbits). **Range and habitat:** widespread throughout the Great Lakes region; in dense brush and weed patches along edges of forest or swamp, with open areas nearby. **Size and weight:** 13 inches; 3 pounds. **Diet:** green vegetation, bark, twigs. **Sounds:** usually silent; loud squeal when extremely distressed.

Cottontails are the pudgy, adorable rabbits with cottonball tails, known to us all from childhood tales of Peter Rabbit. Active day and night, year round, they're generally plentiful due in part to the fact that each adult female produces three or four litters of four to seven young rabbits every year. Of course, a variety of predators helps control their numbers, and few live more than a year in the wild.

Cottontail tracks are easily recognized because the basic pattern doesn't vary much, regardless of the rabbit's speed. It's important to note that, as with all rabbit-family tracks, sometimes the front feet land together, side by side, but just as often the second fore foot lands in line ahead of the first. The eastern cottontail leaves track clusters that span 5 and 12 inches normally, with up to 3 feet between running clusters.

Eastern Cottontail
life size in snow

WHITE-TAILED JACKRABBIT
Jackass rabbit

Lepus townsendi

Order: Lagomorpha (rabbitlike mammals). **Family:** Leporidae (hares and rabbits). **Range and habitat:** Minnesota, Wisconsin, and northern Illinois; in open grassy fields and plains. **Size and weight:** 20 inches; 6 pounds. **Diet:** mostly grasses and other green vegetation, often along highway edges; also shrubs, buds, bark, twigs, and cultivated crops. **Sounds:** normally silent.

The white-tailed jackrabbit, the largest member of the rabbit family in the Great Lakes region, is easily recognized by its long ears, long legs and year-round white fur patch on top of its tail. It is most active from dusk to dawn and spends most of its days lying in depressions it scoops out at the base of a bush, by a rock, or at any other spot that gives it a bit of protection. These jackrabbits are sociable and are often seen feeding in small groups. The white-tailed jackrabbit grows an entirely white or mottled off-white fur coat in winter.

The tracks of the white-tailed jackrabbit are easy to identify. Front prints, about 3 inches long, are usually compact but often splayed, as shown, and fall behind the rear, a pattern typical of all rabbits. Hind prints vary greatly in size. Walking slowly and flat-footed, jackrabbits leave narrow rear prints about 6 inches long, but as speed increases, heels lift until, at top speed of 35 to 40 miles per hour, only the toes leave prints, about 3.5 inches long, sometimes resembling coyote tracks.

Jackrabbit tracks cannot be confused with those of the snowshoe hare, which overlaps the ranges of jackrabbits, because the hare prefers forested rather than open terrain and because its toes are bigger and usually spread apart leaving larger imprints.

The most distinguishing track characteristic of jackrabbits is that, at speed, they leap from 7 to 12 feet or more. Coyotes and snowshoe hares rarely leap more than 6 feet, and cottontails bound no more than 3 feet.

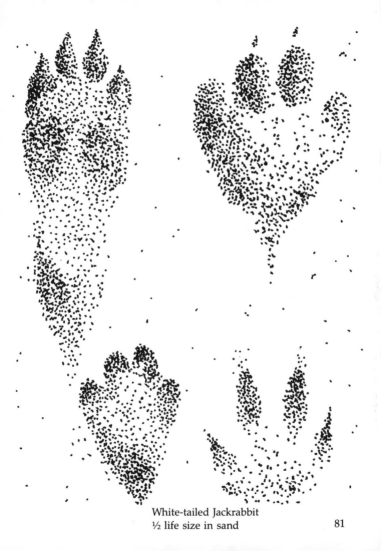

White-tailed Jackrabbit
½ life size in sand

SNOWSHOE HARE
Varying hare

Lepus americanus

Order: Lagomorpha (rabbitlike mammals). **Family:** Leporidae (hares and rabbits). **Range and habitat:** northern half of Minnesota, Wisconsin, and Michigan; also western New York and Pennsylvania; in upland forests, brush thickets, and swamp fringes. **Size and weight:** 18 inches; 4 pounds. **Diet:** succulent vegetation in summer, twigs, bark, and buds in winter; occasionally eats frozen meat. **Sounds:** generally silent; may thump feet, scream, grunt, or growl occasionally.

This medium-sized member of the rabbit family is active day and night year round and is quite common over a large territory within its preferred habitat. The animal has two color phases: medium brown in summer months, molting in winter to white—sometimes slightly mottled with brown—with black ear tips. Aptly named, its unique heavily furred hind feet have separable toes, allowing them to function like snowshoes when the hare is traveling on soft surfaces, especially deep snow.

Although its range partially overlaps that of the cottontail and jackrabbit, track recognition is easy because of the natural snowshoe formed by its toes. A snowshoe hare's toes always spread out, leaving distinctively separate imprints. The length of each track cluster of four prints averages 11 inches; hopping distance is about 14 inches, and leaps are more than 5 feet.

Snowshoe Hare
½ life size in snow

83

TURTLES
Order: Testudines.

Forty-eight species of turtles live in North America. Their tracks are fairly common near bodies of water and, less frequently, in moist woodlands. These peculiar creatures predate dinosaurs and have a body structure unlike any other animal: a shell composed of expanded ribs, limbs extending from within the turtle's rib cage, and a horny beak instead of teeth. The shell is divided into two parts: the upper is called the carapace, and the lower, which is hinged in some species, is called the plastron.

The track left by a turtle is determined by the shape of the plastron and how high the turtle is holding its shell from the ground surface, which in turn depends on the species of turtle, the length of its legs, and the firmness of the surface it's walking over.

The track drawn on the left (the turtle moved toward the top of the page) shows that the turtle dragged most of its plastron, leaving a trail that obscured a lot of the indistinct prints left by its appendages; the drag trail looks similar to that of a tail-dragging beaver, but the shell-dragging turtle trail goes straight for several feet or more, until the turtle changes direction, whereas the beaver's tail-dragging trail zigzags slightly every 6 or 8 inches.

The second turtle trail, drawn on the right, was left on a firmer surface by a turtle who held its plastron off the surface; only the turtle's tail dragged, leaving a narrow, almost straight line. Individual footprints were merely smudges in some places, where the reptile had slipped, but where the turtle took firm steps, the tracks showed its feet and strong claws.

Several turtle species live in the Great Lakes states, including the spiny softshell, Blanding's, eastern box, map, painted, musk, and snapping turtles. All but the snapping turtle leave trails less than 6 inches wide.

Turtles
1/10 life size in mud

BEAVER

Castor canadensis

Order: Rodentia (gnawing mammals). **Family:** Castoridae (beavers). **Range and habitat:** throughout the Great Lakes region; in marshes, streams and lakes with brush and trees or in open forest along riverbanks. **Size and weight:** 36 inches; 55 pounds. **Diet:** aquatic plants, bark, and the twigs and leaves of many shrubs and trees, preferably alder, cottonwood, and willow. **Sounds:** nonvocal, but smacks tail on water surface quite loudly to signal danger.

This industrious, aquatic mammal is the largest North American rodent. Although it sometimes lives unobtrusively in a riverbank, usually it constructs the familiar beaver lodge, a roughly conical pile of brush, stones, and mud extending as much as 6 feet above the surface of a pond, and gnaws down dozens of small softwood trees with which it constructs a conspicuous system of dams, often several hundred yards long. A beaver can grasp objects with its front paws and stand and walk upright on its hind feet. It uses its flat, scaly, strong tail for support out of water and as a rudder when swimming. Gregarious animals, beavers work well together on their collective projects. They are active day and night year round, but may operate unobserved beneath the ice during much of the winter, using subsurface lodge entrances.

If you are lucky, the large, webbed hind foot tracks left by a beaver will be clear, with 6 to 8 inches between pairs. Beavers frequently, however, obscure part or most of their tracks by dragging their tails and/or branches over them, leaving a trail much like that of a 6-inch-wide turtle, except the beaver's tail-drag trail zigzags slightly every 6 or 8 inches. The zigzag is the key to identification, as a turtle moves in reasonably long, straight segments until it changes direction significantly.

Beaver
½ life size in mud

87

MOOSE

Alces alces

Order: Artiodactyla (even-toed hoofed mammals). **Family:** Cervidae (deer). **Range:** parts of Minnesota, Wisconsin, and Michigan; open forests and brushy fields with lakes or swamps, lowland valleys. **Height and weight:** 72 inches at shoulder; 1100 pounds. **Diet:** aquatic plants, leafy succulents, twigs, bark, terminal shoots, and other vegetation. **Sounds:** generally silent, but may make a variety of whines, bellows, grunts, and other guttural noises.

Like all ruminant animals, the moose spends most of its waking hours slowly moving about and chewing. Its normal response to perceived threat is to gallop wildly a few hundred feet on legs wonderfully adapted for running through high, thick brush, then to stop and resume its cud-chewing. Be that as it may, the bull moose does put on quite a display in the autumn, jousting with massive antlers; but beware, it can be quite unpredictably aggressive toward humans at that time of year, as can a cow with a young calf in spring.

You will have no trouble distinguishing moose tracks from those of the much smaller, lighter white-tailed deer. In fact, even moose calves probably leave tracks larger than those of most white-tails. Adult moose tracks are nearly twice as large: 6 inches (with a walking stride of 4 feet), compared to about 3.5 inches for a full-grown white-tailed deer.

Finally, the moose is not a herd animal. A moose gathering is generally no larger than a bull, cow, and two calves, whereas white-tailed deer may congregate in larger numbers. Then again, a few moose can make a lot of tracks hanging around a small pond for an extended period of time, which they do. In that case, though, the largeness of the adult tracks will provide positive identification.

Moose
½ life size in mud

BLACK BEAR   *Ursus americanus*

Order: Carnivora (flesh-eating mammals). **Family:** Ursidae (bears).
Range and habitat: parts of northern Minnesota, Wisconsin, and
Michigan; primarily in upland forests and swamp fringes. **Size and
weight:** 6.5 feet; 450 pounds. **Diet:** omnivorous, including smaller
mammals, fish, carrion, insects, fruit, berries, nuts, and succulent
plants. **Sounds:** usually silent, but may growl, grunt, woof, whimper,
click teeth, smack jaws together, or make other immediately recognizable indications of annoyance or alarm.

The black bear is the smallest and most common American bear.
You may have seen these animals around rural garbage dumps and in
parks. In the wild, the black bear is shy and wary of human contact as
a general rule and thus not frequently sighted. If you do sight one,
however, it can be very dangerous to underestimate it. The black bear
is very strong, agile, and quick. It climbs trees, swims well, can run
25 miles per hour for short stretches, and above all else, is unpredict-
able. The black bear may seem docile and harmless in parks, but it
has been known to chase people with great determination.

Be alert for bear trails, worn deep by generations of bears, and for
trees with claw marks and other indications of bear territory. Bear
tracks are usually easy to identify; they are roughly human in shape
and size but slightly wider. The large claws leave prints wherever the
toes do. If a bear slips on mud or ice, its soles leave distinctive
smooth slide marks; nearby you will no doubt find more orderly
tracks. Adult black bear tracks measure about 7 inches.

Black Bear
½ life size in mud

Birds

NORTHERN JUNCO

Junco hyemalis

Order: Passeriformes (perching birds). **Family:** Fringillidae (buntings, finches, and sparrows). **Range and habitat:** summers in Minnesota, Wisconsin and Michigan; winters in Illinois and Indiana; year-round resident of Ohio, Pennsylvania, and New York; common in and near coniferous forests, weedy fields, brushy forest fringes. **Size and weight:** length 6 inches, wingspan 8 inches; less than 1 ounce. **Diet:** seeds, insects, and berries. **Sounds:** chips and trills.

The junco is a common and wide-ranging little bird. Small flocks of slate-colored juncos moving about in search of seeds on the surface of winter snow are a common sight throughout nearly all of the Great Lakes states, as is the network of interlaced tracks these and other small birds leave beneath bird feeders. Juncos are attracted to the seeds that chickadees scatter while looking for sunflower seeds in the standard wild bird mix; they may be accompanied by an occasional sparrow during their winter outings.

Junco tracks are typical of the vast number of smaller land birds that leave delicate lines on snow, sand, or mud of inland areas. Hind toes are about twice as long as front toes, and the tracks are found in pairs spaced up to 5 inches apart, as these birds hop instead of walk. The relative size of the tracks will give a clue to the identity of the maker, as will habitat and seasonal considerations, verified, of course, by actual field sightings.

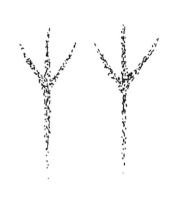

Northern Junco
life size in snow

KILLDEER

Charadrius vociferus

Order: Charadriiformes (shorebirds, gulls, and terns). **Family:** Charadriidae (plovers). **Range and habitat:** year-round south of Lake Erie, summers northward; common along shorelines, also found on inland fields and pastures. **Size and weight:** length 8 inches, wingspan 12 inches; 4 ounces. **Diet:** insects and larvae, earthworms, seeds, **Sounds:** repeats its name as its call.

The killdeer is one of the most common and recognizable shorebirds. Its two black breast bands are distinctive, as is its habit of feigning injury to lead intruders away from its nesting area. The killdeer is the only shorebird found year round in most of the region. Its tracks are typical as well of the tracks—usually found on damp sand—of shorebirds that visit the region seasonally: the front center toe is longer than the two outer toes; the small hind toe, more of a heel spur than a toe, leaves a small imprint; and the tracks are usually printed in a line, only an inch or two apart for birds the size of the killdeer, less for sandpipers, and up to 6 inches for birds the size of a greater yellowlegs. The general shape and lack of any evidence of webbing between the toes separate shorebird tracks from those of gulls or ducks.

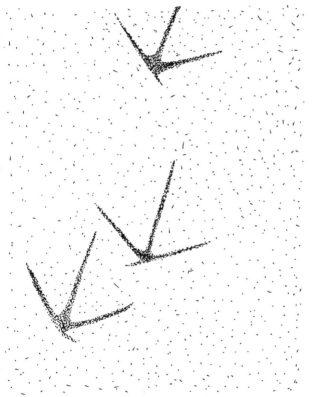

Killdeer
life size in sand

RUFFED GROUSE   *Bonasa umbellus*

Order: Galliformes (land-living game birds). **Family:** Tetraonidae (grouse). **Range and habitat:** year-round resident of Great Lakes region, except absent from prairie portions of Illinois and Indiana; clearings in and near wooded areas in summer, winters in evergreen forests. **Size and weight:** length, 14 inches; wingspan, 16 inches; weight, 2 pounds. **Diet:** seeds, insects. **Sounds:** while on the ground, male creates a drumming sound with wings as part of autumn courting ritual.

The ruffed grouse is a mottled, grayish-brown, chickenlike game bird. It's fairly widespread; you've probably seen it strutting along the edges of country roads as often as anywhere else. The tail of both sexes ends in several brown bands and one black band; the male commonly displays the tail fanned like a hand of cards. Typical of its land-living, game-bird cousins, ruffed grouse are nonmigratory and spend most of their lives on the ground. When threatened, they prefer to run and hide; as a last resort, they burst into full flight with rapid beats of their short, rounded wings, fly away fairly quickly, and return to earth within a few hundred feet.

The ruffed grouse tracks illustrated are also representative of the spruce grouse, gray partridge, ring-necked pheasant, and northern bobwhite, locally common from farmlands to forest around the Great Lakes. All these birds have feet particularly adapted for life on the ground: the fourth toe is not as well developed as the front three; it may leave a small impression directly behind the middle toe or angling slightly toward the center of the trail; more often than not, it leaves no mark at all. Tracks for these birds will range in size from about 1.5 inches for the bobwhite to over 2 inches for the ring-necked pheasant. At first glance you might think you're looking at shorebird tracks, but the toes of these upland birds are distinctly thicker and the heels larger.

Ruffed Grouse
life size in mud

AMERICAN CROW

Corvus brachyrhynchos

Order: Passeriformes (perching birds). **Family:** Corvidae (jays, magpies, crows). **Range and habitat:** year-round throughout the Great Lakes region; in all habitats. **Size and weight:** length 17 inches, wingspan 26 inches; 1 pound. **Diet:** nearly everything from mice to carrion to garbage. **Sounds:** distinctive "caw."

Crows are relatively intelligent birds, quite vocal, make good pets and can be taught to mimic human voices. Researchers have also determined that crows can count, and both wild and pet crows have been observed making up games to play. Watching crows will often help you locate other wildlife, too: groups of crows will mob and scold a predator such as an owl, for example, or perch near an offensive animal, darting in to harrass and scold it. The common crow can be told from a distant hawk by its frequent steady flapping; it seldom glides more than 2 or 3 seconds except in strong updrafts or when descending.

All four of the crow's toes are about the same length, each with a strong claw, all of which leaves prints most of the time. Crows walk and skip; their tracks are not usually made in pairs.

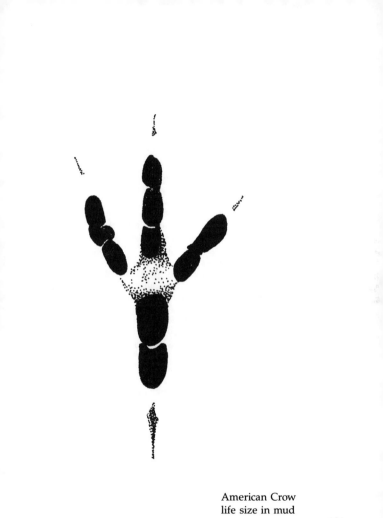

American Crow
life size in mud

101

MALLARD

Anas platyrynchos

Order: Anseriformes. **Family:** Anatidae (ducks, geese and swans).
Range and habitat: summer or year-round resident throughout the
Great Lakes region; lakes, ponds, fresh-water marshes, and coastal
waters. **Size and weight:** length 28 inches, wingspan 40 inches; 3.5
pounds. **Diet:** grains, insects, and small aquatic plants, insects, mol-
lusks and fish. **Sounds:** a loud quack.

The mallard resides year round in much of the Great Lakes region
and is easily recognized by its blue speculum (wing band) and, in the
male, emerald-green head, white neck-band, and rusty-colored
breast. The wide-ranging mallards are usually seen in the wild, dab-
bling and tipping in the shallows of fresh- and saltwater bodies, but
they are not shy around humans and are often found waiting
patiently for handouts around park ponds, waterfront cafes, and similar civilized habitat. In water they rarely dive; in flight they are agile
and take off nearly vertically.

The tracks are typical of all waterfowl, as well as coastal birds, including all seagulls, cormorants, terns, shearwaters, petrels, gannet,
jaegers, and the alcids (razorbills, murres, dovekie, guillemots, and
puffins). All these birds have hind toes so small and elevated that
they do not leave imprints. The three main toes fan out in front and
are connected by webs, which nearly always leave prints. Tracks like
these will range in size from somewhat less than 2 inches long for
small ducks to 7 inches for whistling swans. Once again, with tracks
as initial clues, patient field work and an intimate knowledge of the
species frequenting the area at the time of year the tracks are found
will allow you to accurately guess the track makers' identity.

Mallard
life size in mud

GREAT HORNED OWL   *Bubo virginianus*
Cat owl

Order: Strigiformes (owls). **Family:** Strigidae (owls). **Range and habitat:** year-round throughout Great Lakes region; widespread and adaptable, from forests to meadows to cliff faces. **Size and weight:** length 24 inches, wingspan 48 inches; 3.5 pounds. **Diet:** rabbits, mice, rats, voles, skunks, and grouse. **Sounds:** males normally hoot four or five times in sequence, females six to eight times.

This common, large, "eared" owl does look catlike when it sits staring at you from a lofty perch or nesting tree. The male and female prefer to use nests constructed in previous years by hawks or ravens rather than building their own, and they nest so early in spring that the brooding female is often partially covered with snow. Special modifications of its wing feathers allow this night hunter to drop silently onto the back of unsuspecting prey.

The shape of the tracks illustrated is representative of numerous species of owls inhabiting the Great Lakes region. Owl tracks are uncommon except in snow country, where an owl may leave a few tracks around a kill site or when it lands to investigate and feed on food too heavy to carry away. You may also find owl tracks on recently rained-upon dirt roads where an owl has discovered a car-killed animal.

The tracks of the great horned owl in mud show its three thick, powerful toes and imprints of its long, sharp talons. The hind toe mark is always insignificant or absent. Smaller owl species obviously leave smaller tracks. Unless you are lucky enough to see these smaller owls in the act of making tracks, there's no way to identify the tracks by species. You might get a clue by observing the area at dusk, the best time for sighting owls, to see what species are present in the vicinity of the tracks you have found.

Great Horned Owl
life size in mud

GREAT BLUE HERON   *Ardea herodias*

Order: Ciconiiformes (herons and allies). **Family:** Ardeidae (herons, egrets, and bitterns). **Range and habitat:** widespread summer or year-round; in most lowland areas, common on freshwater and ocean shores. **Size and weight:** length 48 inches, wingspan 72 inches; 7 pounds. **Diet:** fish, snakes, insects, mice, and frogs. **Sounds:** "kraak" and strident honks.

The presence of a great blue heron magically transforms an aquatic landscape, adding an aura of quiet elegance characteristic of the best Oriental brush paintings. This large heron typically walks slowly through shallows or stands with head hunched on shoulders, looking for the fish that make up a large part of its diet. A heron's nest, maintained year after year, is an elaborate structure of sticks 3 feet across built in a tree; the great blue herons often nest colonially.

You will most often find great blue heron tracks bordering the freshwater areas where the bird feeds. The four toes and claws of each foot usually leave visible imprints. The well-developed hind toe enables the heron to stand for long periods of time on one leg or the other or to walk very slowly while hunting.

This track shape is typical of all the herons, egrets, bitterns, cranes, rails, and American coot found in the Great Lakes states. The size and location of the tracks will vary according to species.

Great Blue Heron
life size in mud

Recommended Reading

CARE OF THE WILD FEATHERED AND FURRED: A Guide to Wildlife Handling and Care, Mae Hickman and Maxine Guy (Unity Press, 1973); unique perspectives on animal behavior and emergency care of injured and orphaned wildlife.

A FIELD GUIDE TO ANIMAL TRACKS, Olaus J. Murie (Houghton Mifflin Co., Boston, 2nd ed., 1975); a classic work on track identification by Murie (1889–1963), an eminent naturalist and wildlife artist; one of the Peterson Field Guide Series; an excellent research text for home study.

ISLAND SOJOURN, Elizabeth Arthur (Harper & Row, 1980); an account of life on an island in British Columbia's wilderness, with a chapter devoted to a metaphysical perspective of animal tracks.

SNOW TRACKS, Jean George (E. P. Dutton, 1958); an introduction to the study of animal tracks for very young children.

THE TRACKER, Tom Brown and William J. Watkins (Berkley Publications, 1984); an intriguing story by a man who has devoted his life to the science of following tracks and other movement clues of various animals, including humans.

Index

About the author:

Chris Stall first became interested in wild country and wild animals during several years with a very active Boy Scout troop in rural New York State, where he spent his youth. In the two decades since then he has travelled and lived around most of North America, studying, photographing, sketching and writing about wild animals in their natural habitats. His photos and articles have appeared in a number of outdoor and nature magazines.

Collect ANIMAL TRACKS books and posters for other regions of the country!

For your own travels, or for gifts to friends and relatives in other regions, look for these fine books and matching posters at your nearby book, nature or out-door stores, or order direct from the publisher.

BOOKS are all the same size and format as the one you hold in your hand, ready for pocket, pack or glove compartment. $5.95 each.

POSTERS are large (25" × 38"), top-quality, two-color posters richly printed on heavy stock. Each shows most of the same 40–50 tracks from the matching book. Every poster is a different color for display as a set. $5.95 each.

Areas available:

GREAT LAKES	PACIFIC NORTHWEST
MID-ATLANTIC	ROCKY MOUNTAINS
NEW ENGLAND	CALIFORNIA

Order toll-free with VISA / MasterCard—1-800-553-4453—or send check or money order. Add $2.00 per order for shipping and handling, **plus** *$1.50 if your order includes a poster:*

THE MOUNTAINEERS
1001 S.W. Klickitat Way
Seattle, WA   98134